First Questions and Answers about Buildings

Do Buildings Have Bones?

TIME LIFE for Children®

ALEXANDRIA, VIRGINIA

Contents

How long does it take to build a house?

A long time! Building a house is a big job. First, people must find a good place to build it. Then plans and drawings are made that show how the house will look. Finally, builders work for many months inside and outside. Everything must be just right before a family moves into its new home.

5

How do the builders know where all the rooms go?

They follow a plan. Before a house is built, a person called an architect makes a special drawing of it. The drawing is called a blueprint. It tells the workers where to build the basement, the roof, and all the rooms in between. Every wall, ceiling, floor, door, and window is in the architect's plan.

LIVING ROOM

Why are basements at the bottom of houses?

A house is very heavy. It needs a solid bottom, or foundation, so it doesn't sink into the ground. To make the foundation, workers dig a hole with a flat bottom. They pour concrete into it to make it smooth, hard, and strong.

If the house has a basement, the workers pour more concrete into wooden frames to make the basement walls, or they make walls out of concrete blocks.

Did you know?
The back of a concrete truck turns to keep the concrete mixed up inside.

9

Who builds the walls?

Carpenters bring tools and wood to build the walls, floors, and ceilings. Soon the sound of buzzing saws and banging hammers fills the air.

First carpenters lay a wooden floor. Then they measure and cut boards for each wall. They nail the boards together to make a frame. When the frame matches the architect's blueprint, they stand it up and nail it in place. One by one the sides of the house go up.

Hey, that tickles!

Did you know?
Carpenters cover the outside of the house with big, flat pieces of wood called plywood.

11

Why do we need a roof on top?

A roof protects a house from rain and snow. It keeps everyone and everything inside the house dry.

First workers build a wooden frame.

Then they nail plywood boards to the frame.

Next they lay special paper on the plywood. This keeps the wood dry.

Did you know?

Each shingle on the roof covers a bit of the one below it. Rain can't get between the shingles. Instead of soaking into the roof, the water runs off it.

Finally they nail shingles one by one onto the roof.

How do the windows fit in?

From the basement to the rooftop, workers have left spaces for windows. Now it is time to add them. The builders get windows and doors from a factory. They fit them snugly into the empty spaces. Workers use a tool called a level to make sure the windows and doors are put in straight.

Try it!

Place a marble on a window frame. If the marble sits still, the window is level. If it rolls, the frame is tilted.

Who builds the chimney?

Workers called masons build the chimney with bricks and cement. First they lay down a row of bricks. Then they spread on wet cement and stack more bricks on top in an overlapping pattern. The masons keep adding layers of bricks and cement until the chimney is done. When the cement dries, it hold the bricks together and makes the chimney strong.

Did you know?

Bricks are made of clay that is dug out of the earth. The clay is shaped like blocks and baked to make it hard and strong.

17

Where are those wires going?

They will bring electricity to every room in the house. Workers called electricians put wires inside the walls. They slip them through holes in the wooden frame and slide them between floors and ceilings. One end of each wire goes to a thick cable that brings electricity into the house. The other end goes to a box with a switch. The switch turns the electricity on and off.

Did you know?
Electrical outlets and wires are not playthings. Be sure to stay away from them!

What are all those pipes for?

They carry water to sinks, toilets, and bathtubs in the house. Thin copper pipes bring in fresh water for cooking, cleaning, and drinking. Thicker white plastic pipes carry away dirty wastewater. Plumbers place the pipes inside the walls and under the floors. They connect them so that water can flow into and out of the house without leaking.

Peekaboo!

Did you know?

Not all pipes carry water. In some houses, pipes bring gas into the house for cooking or heating.

What keeps a house warm?

Many houses stay warm using a furnace. The furnace is a big metal box that sits in the basement or on the first floor. Some furnaces use gas or oil to heat air. Others boil water until it turns to steam. The hot air or steam goes up through special passageways to heat every room in the house.

Did you know?
Builders put special padding called insulation in walls, under floors, and in ceilings. Like a warm sweater, the insulation helps hold heat in the house.

23

Can a house move?

Sometimes a house is moved from one place to another. It takes lots of people and machines to do the job!

First a plumber and an electrician stop water and electricity from flowing into the house. Next workers dig a deep ditch around the house and cut it off its concrete foundation. Then machines lift the house carefully onto a trailer. A truck slowly tows the house to its new location.

Here we go!

Why do houses look so different?

One reason is because people like different kinds of architecture, or building styles. Another is because there are so many different materials from which to choose:

Boards or shingles cover wooden houses.

Stones from the earth are cemented together to make stone houses.

Hundreds of small clay bricks are needed for brick houses.

Log cabins are made by stacking tree trunks.

Adobe houses are made of sunbaked mud bricks.

27

Why is that lighthouse so tall?

Its tall tower has a big light at the very top. The light shines far out to sea to warn ships that land is near.

Long ago a lighthouse keeper lived in the lighthouse and worked the light. Nowadays computers turn the light beam on and off.

29

Why is this house on poles?

Houses on the beach are built to be safe in case strong ocean waves sweep over the sand. That's why they are often built on poles, called stilts. In a storm, water goes under the house, not in it.

31

Are castles real?

Yes, they are. Castles are like big forts. They were built long ago to protect noblemen, their families, and their soldiers. Masons cut and shaped large bricks or stones for the castle walls. Workers carried the stones and put them in place one by one.

Old castles can still be found in a few countries, but you may have to travel a very long distance to see one!

Why is grass growing on that roof?

Because the house is built into the earth. Underground houses are usually dug into the side of a hill. The earth around the house helps keep it warm in winter and cool in summer. Earth may cover the roof, too. Can you imagine growing grass on your roof?

35

Why aren't greenhouses green?

The house isn't green, but the things inside it are! A green-house is the perfect place to grow flowers and plants. Sunlight shines through its clear walls and roof to warm the plants and help them grow.

Sometimes a greenhouse gets too hot for the plants inside it. Then the doors or flaps in the roof must be opened to cool things off.

37

How does that giant roof stay up?

Most stadiums are open on top. But some have huge dome roofs that keep out rain and snow. Steel bars make a frame for the roof. They connect in a pattern that looks like a giant spider web. Each part of the web is covered with a steel panel. Foam and plastic are laid over the top to make the dome waterproof.

SUPERDOME TONIGHT!

HAMMERS VS. RAZERS

Do buildings have bones?

In a way they do. The bones in your body make up your skeleton. They give your body its shape and make it strong.

Tall buildings have a skeleton, too. Their "bones" are bars of steel called girders. These steel bones hold up the walls, floors, and ceilings. Girders allow skyscrapers to be very very tall.

How high can a skyscraper go?

Right now, the tallest building in the world is the Sears Tower in Chicago, Illinois. On a clear day, you can see four different states from the top floor!

The buildings of the future may be even higher. People called engineers are working hard to find stronger materials and new ways to make buildings taller and taller.

Empire State Building
New York
1,250 feet

World Trade Center
New York
1,350 feet

Sears Tower
Chicago
1,454 feet

Why are they knocking that building down?

After a long time buildings get old. Some old buildings can be fixed up and used again. Others are knocked down to make room for new buildings. Workers use big trucks to do the job.

First, a tall crane with a heavy iron ball smashes into the tops of walls. Then a clamshell bucket scoops out bricks and rubble. Next bulldozers slam into the building's base. Finally, dump trucks carry away the old building material.

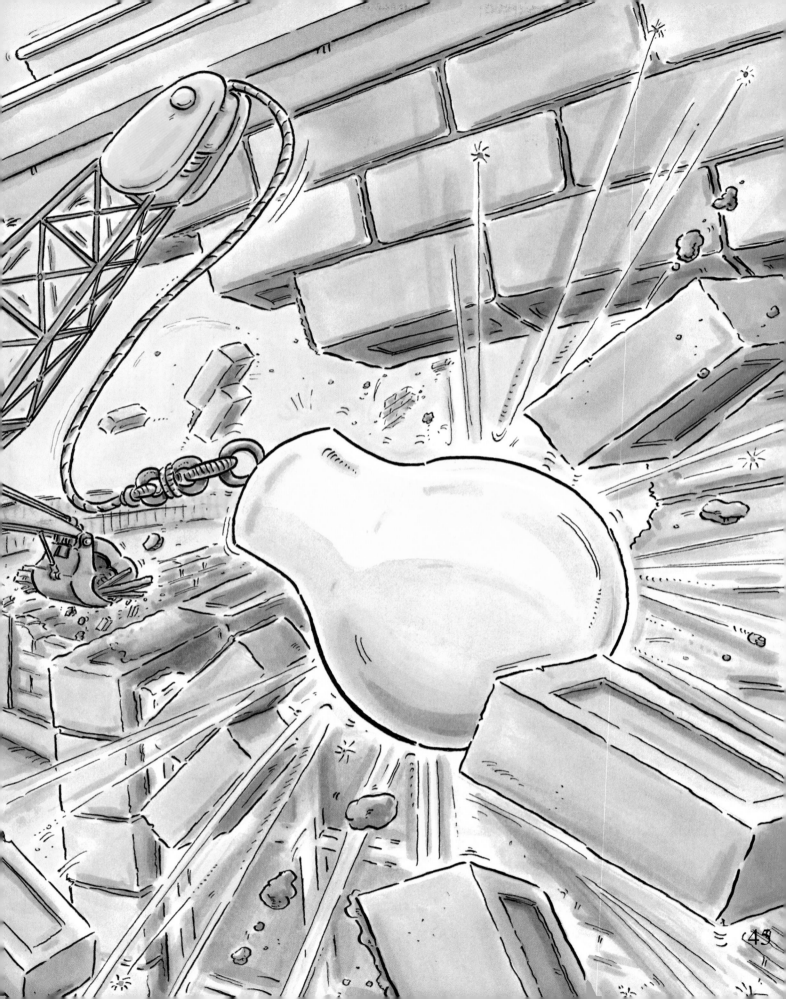

How long will our house last?

A long, long time. If we build them with strong materials and take care of them, houses will last until you are grown up, and even longer.

Home sweet home!

TIME-LIFE for CHILDREN®

Managing Editor: Patricia Daniels
Editorial Directors: Jean Burke Crawford, Allan Fallow,
Sara Mark
Senior Art Director: Susan K. White
Publishing Associate: Marike van der Veen
Administrative Assistant: Mary M. Saxton
Production Manager: Marlene Zack
Quality Assurance Manager: Miriam P. Newton
Library: Louise D. Forstall, Anne Heising

Special Contributors: Barbara Klein, Tom Neven,
Anne E. Parrish
Researcher: Jocelyn Lindsay
Writer: Andrew Gutelle

Designed by: David Bennett Books

Series design: David Bennett
Book design: David Bennett
Art direction: David Bennett
Illustrated by: Michael Reid
**Additional cover
 illustrations by:** Nick Baxter

First printing. Printed in U.S.A.
Published simultaneously in Canada.

Time Life Inc. is a wholly owned subsidiary of THE TIME INC. BOOK COMPANY.

TIME-LIFE is a trademark of Time Warner Inc. U.S.A.
For subscription information, call 1-800-621-7026.

Library of Congress Cataloging-in-Publication Data

Do buildings have bones? : first questions and answers about buildings. p. cm.– (Time-Life library of first questions and answers)
ISBN 0-7835-0900-6 (hardcover)
1. Building–Miscellanea–Juvenile literature. 2. Buildings–Miscellanea–Juvenile literature. [1. Building–Miscellanea.
2. Buildings–Miscellanea. 3. Questions and answers.] I.Time-Life for Children (Firm)
II. Series: Library of first questions and answers.
TH149.D63 1995   94-48260

720—dc20   CIP
                                                                                                                                        AC

Consultants

Dr. Lewis P. Lipsitt, an internationally recognized specialist on childhood development, was the 1990 recipient of the Nicholas Hobbs Award for science in the service of children. He has served as the science director for the American Psychological Association and is a professor of psychology and medical science at Brown University.

Dr. Judith A. Schickedanz, an authority on the education of preschool children, is an associate professor of early childhood education at the Boston University School of Education, where she also directs the Early Childhood Learning Laboratory. Her published work includes *More Than the ABCs: Early Stages of Reading and Writing* as well as several textbooks and many scholarly papers.